...e prison. We have plen... food and fuel, and ar...
...h better treated than one woul... yet,
...thstanding all this, the monotony of a prison life
... trying to my patience. I have no books, ...
..., or any ... which to pass aw...
...dious ho... pass the most of ...
... in sleepi... leased so that I ca...
...ate with ...z to their Country
...tired of ... cursez that an...
...ly hurted ...tez, by the Rebe...
... I trust ... up the Ship ...
...uth iz for ...ion. When you
...me again tell me all about the Mount fam...
...e they are, and what they have been doing sin...
...mmencement of the Rebellion, Tell Cousin Lizz...
...ld be pleased to receive a letter from her. What ...
...ecome of Cousin Tom Seabury, I suppose he haz m...
...iank in the Federal army by this time. I have no...
...from Martha since I last wrote, but am exep...
...a letter every day. I Am Dear Father Your
Affectionate Son
Wm Shep. Mount.

...above iz an exact copy of
...riginal which haz been sent to Washington; to
...Wm Hoffman Commissary Gen. of Prisoners.
L. A. Mount.

MR. LINCOLN'S GIFT

A Civil War Story

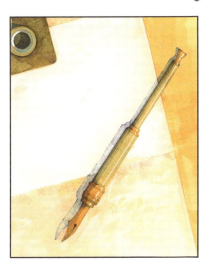

MR. LINCOLN'S GIFT

A Civil War Story

By WHITNEY STEWART

Illustrated by LAINE DUNHAM AKIYAMA

FRIENDS OF HILDENE, PUBLISHER
MANCHESTER, VERMONT 2008

First Edition

Published by Friends of Hildene, Inc.
Post Office Box 377
Manchester, Vermont 05254
802 362-1788
www.hildene.org

Printed and bound by
Springfield Printing Corporation
Springfield, Vermont

Library of Congress Cataloging-in-Publication Data
ISBN13 978-0-9754917-4-4

"If it is the design of Heaven that I shall at last have light and comfort, I can truly say there is no hand from whom I would so joyfully receive it as from the hand of Abraham Lincoln."

—William Mount

AUTHOR'S NOTE

One evening my stepfather handed me a box of old letters and photographs that he inherited from his great, great grandfather, Francis B. Carpenter. I love old letters, so I dug right into the box. I gently pulled out fragile pieces of paper that dated back to the 1800s. And then I realized that these letters were written by famous Americans - poets, artists, newspapermen, and members of Abraham Lincoln's Cabinet. I held my breath because I was excited and read one letter after the other. I read late into the night. These letters told an interesting story.

And I will retell it for you.

The White House was crowded on February 6, 1864. People pushed in line to get close to Abraham Lincoln. The president wore a black suit and white gloves. And he stood taller than all his guests.

Mr. Lincoln greeted the artist Frank Carpenter and shook his hand.

"Do you think, Mr. Carpenter, that you can make a handsome picture of me?" the president asked.

Frank was not sure what to say. Mr. Lincoln was making a joke about his own homely face.

"Mr. President, could we discuss the painting in private?" asked Frank.

"I reckon," Mr. Lincoln said. "Come up to my office when this show is over." And he turned to shake the next guest's hand.

Frank wanted to paint a picture of President Lincoln reading aloud his Emancipation Proclamation to his cabinet members. This proclamation was the beginning of freedom for America's slaves. What better way to record the event than to paint a picture of it? Frank wanted the world to remember that Abraham Lincoln worked for justice and liberty.

The Emancipation Proclamation

On January 1, 1863, during the heat of the Civil War, President Abraham Lincoln issued the Emancipation Proclamation. This proclamation was meant to free the slaves held in the states that fought against the Union. But southern slaveholders had no intention of obeying Lincoln's proclamation. Many slaves did not hear of the emancipation until long after its issue. Freedom came slowly. The emancipation was the beginning of liberty, but slavery was not fully abolished in the United States until the Thirteenth Constitutional Amendment of 1865.

Frank had a job to do at the White House. But he also had a promise to keep - a promise to save a young soldier named William Mount. William was dying in a Civil War prison. But he said he was an innocent victim of war. William's father begged Frank to ask the president for help.

The Civil War hurt many families. Frank's brother, William Carpenter, was shot in the leg at Gettysburg, Pennsylvania. And he died of gangrene. Frank could not save his own brother. But perhaps he could save William Mount. He waited for the right moment to talk to Mr. Lincoln. Until then, he worked on his painting.

"I've never felt stronger about a painting in my life," Frank told the president.

He set up a giant canvas in the State Dining Room.

Frank sat quietly in Mr. Lincoln's office and sketched the president's face. The gray shadows under Mr. Lincoln's eyes and the deep creases in his cheeks told Frank that the president didn't eat or sleep well. And he worked long hours. Lincoln was troubled by the war's death toll, and he wanted the fighting to end.

"The president has the saddest face I've ever seen,"
Frank thought.

Then Frank sketched Lincoln's seven cabinet members. But the men grew impatient. Like the president, they couldn't sit around all day for a painter. They had a country to run. So Frank had to continue sketching the men from photographs before he worked on his big canvas.

~14~

Frank outlined the eight men in chalk on the canvas. Then he drew their eyes, head shapes, and faces in pencil. He sketched, erased, and re-sketched until he was satisfied. Next, he mixed his paints - a serious black for the men's clothing, a red-brown for the wooden furniture, and a warm yellow for the room. He stroked his brush against the canvas and stood back to judge his work.

From time to time Mr. Lincoln poked his head into the room to watch Frank's progress. "Carry on. Carry on," he said.

Each night Frank painted until long after the president had climbed into bed. Sometimes he couldn't break the spell that held him while he painted. And he forgot to sleep. But he never forgot his promise to help William Mount.

"Don't bother Mr. Lincoln now," Frank kept telling himself whenever he saw the president.

Then one evening, Frank found the president at the top of his private staircase. Frank wanted to say something, but he felt awkward. He almost kept quiet. But he changed his mind.

"Mr. President," Frank said. "I have a personal request; may I ask a few moments of your time?"

President Lincoln thought for a moment and said, "Come upstairs by and by, and we can fix it up."

Chandeliers brightened the president's office. The two men sat at a long table facing each other. Mr. Lincoln's eyes sagged. He was tired, but he listened. Frank told the story of William Mount.

William grew up in the north. But, he moved to Mississippi to escape cold winters because of his delicate health. In the south, he married a young woman and had a child. The Civil War broke out, and William was made to join the Confederate army against his will. He didn't want to fight his friends in the North. He believed in freedom for slaves and union for the country.

William marched with the Confederate troops until he became sick. He wheezed and coughed and could go no further. And he was sent to the hospital and put to bed. Outside, deadly battles shredded his country. Inside, William planned his escape.

The American Civil War
1861 - 1865

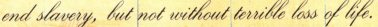

The Civil War was also called the "War Between the States." The Union of the United States of America, led by Abraham Lincoln and the Republican Party, was in conflict with the Confederate states of the south under Jefferson Davis. The Union opposed the expansion of slavery into United States territories. The Confederacy wanted to keep slavery legal, and the southern states broke away from the Union. Lincoln saw this action as a rebellion.

The fighting started on April 12, 1861 when the Confederate Army attacked Fort Sumter in South Carolina. Lincoln formed an army to fight back and save the Union. In the next four years, America suffered through some of the worst battles in American history. More than six hundred thousand soldiers and unknown thousands of civilians died. In the end, Lincoln was able to save the Union and end slavery, but not without terrible loss of life.

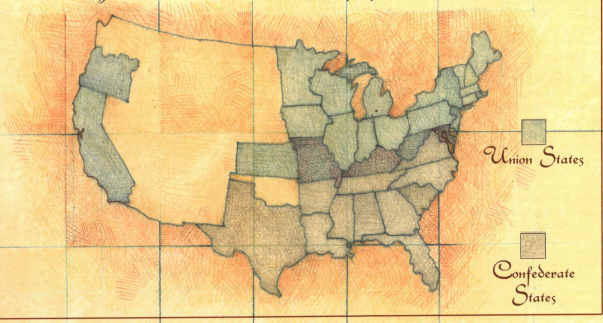

Union States

Confederate States

William got better and rejoined his troops, but not for long. Near Vicksburg he snuck away and gave himself up to Union officers. He told them he was a northerner. But the officers thought he was a rebel spy and threw him in jail. William's cough deepened, and he grew thin and pale. He was wasting away behind locked doors, and nobody believed his story.

William's father asked Frank to explain all this to the president. Mr. Lincoln heard petitions like this every week. He had to decide the fate of many men. Some of them lied for their freedom. "That will do," he told Frank.

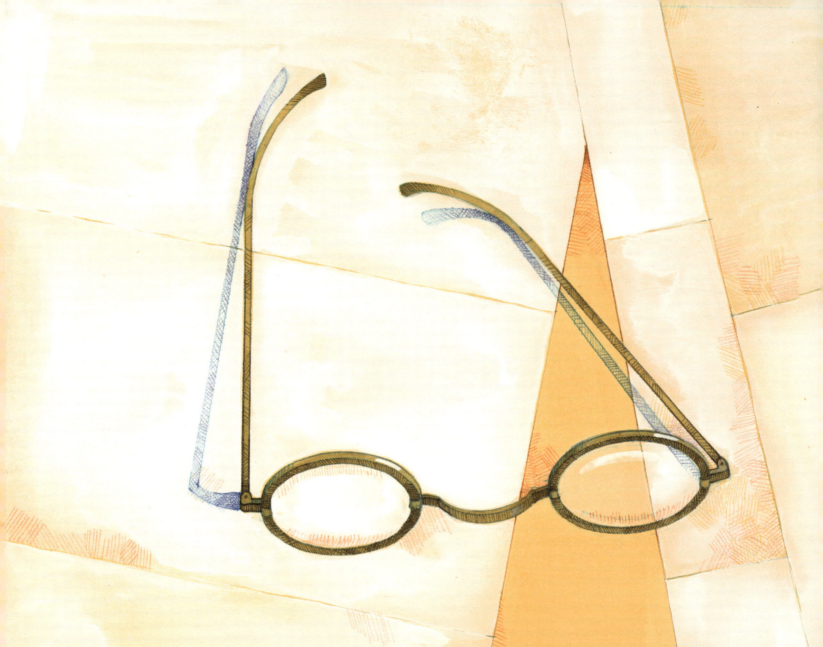

Frank was silent. What would the president say next?

Mr. Lincoln looked Frank in the eyes. "Do you know this man and his son so well that you can vouch for their loyalty?"

"I do not know the young man," Frank admitted. "But the father - there's no truer patriot or better man."

Mr. Lincoln nodded and wrote a note. There was no sound in the room but the scratching of his pen. Frank looked up at the president and then down at the message.

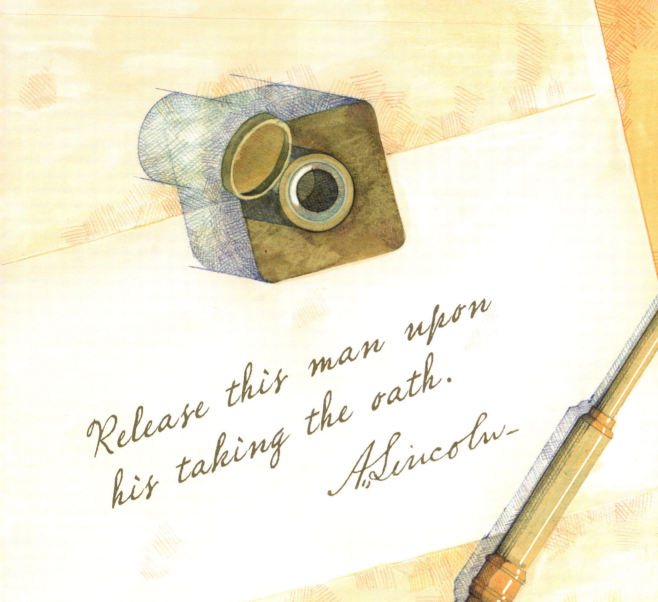

Release this man upon his taking the oath.

A. Lincoln—

"There, that will do it." Mr. Lincoln told Frank. "You can take that over to the War Department yourself and have it telegraphed tonight to the prison at Alton. You will find it all right. The young man will be released tomorrow morning."

Frank smiled. William Mount could go free, and the artist could finish his painting.

The following morning Frank dabbed and swished his brush across his canvas. He thought of President Lincoln and the two young soldiers named William. For his brother, William Carpenter, life had ended in war. But for William Mount, justice and liberty were Mr. Lincoln's gift

AFTERWORD

This story and all of the dialogue is documented in Frank Carpenter's private diary and personal letters, in magazine articles that he wrote, and in his book originally entitled *Six Months at the White House with Abraham Lincoln: The Story of a Picture.*

Frank Carpenter titled his painting "The First Reading of the Emancipation Proclamation Before the Cabinet." After Lincoln was assassinated, Frank exhibited the painting around the country. Thousands of mourners went to see it. The painting now hangs in the Senate wing of the US Capitol Building.

ABRAHAM LINCOLN

    Abraham Lincoln was the sixteenth president of the United States. He was born near Hodgenville, Kentucky on February 12, 1809, in a log cabin. Big for his age, Lincoln helped his father work on family land in Kentucky, Indiana, and Illinois. At the age of twenty-three, Lincoln ran for a government office. He was defeated, but his taste for serving the people remained. On November 6, 1860, Lincoln was elected as America's new president. Five months later, the Civil War began, and the country was torn apart. Lincoln spent his first term trying to end the war and free America's slaves. He was reelected in 1864 but did not serve out his second term. On April 14, 1865, the disturbed actor John Wilkes Booth assassinated Lincoln in Washington's Ford's Theater. Lincoln was buried near his home in Springfield, Illinois.

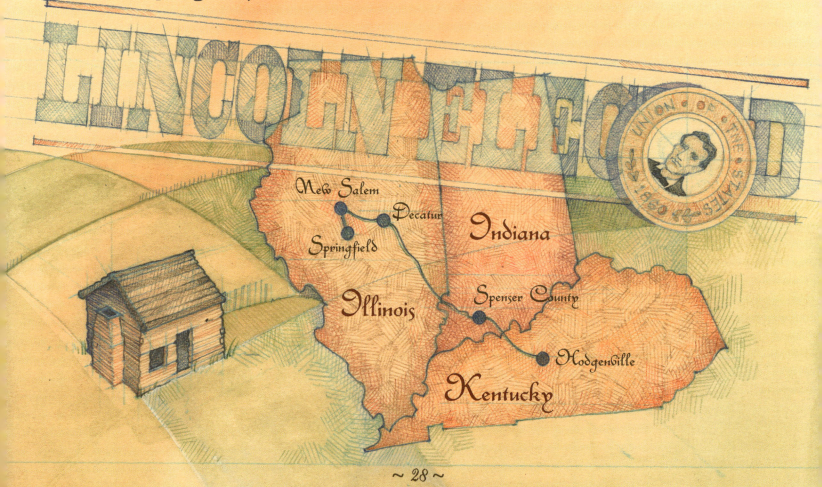

FRANCIS B. CARPENTER

Francis B. Carpenter was born in 1830 in Homer, New York. As a child, he dreamed of being an artist. He spent six months as an apprentice to a professional painter. At age fifteen, he opened his own art studio in Homer. He painted portraits of local families. Six years later he moved to New York City and opened a bigger studio. Before he died in 1900, he painted five United States presidents and dozens of famous men and women.

WILLIAM MOUNT

William Shepard Mount was born into a family of artists of New York State. His father, Shepard Alonzo Mount, two uncles, an aunt, and a cousin were all well-known American painters. At the time of his imprisonment, William was married and had one child. After Frank Carpenter delivered Lincoln's message to the War Department, William Mount was released from the Union prison in Alton, Illinois.

AUTHOR ACKNOWLEDGEMENTS

I thank my stepfather, A. George Scherer III, for showing me Frank Carpenter's letters and helping me gather research material. (George is Frank's great, great grandson.) George's mother and Carpenter's great grandaughter, Clara Scherer, spent hours telling me about her ancestors. My mother, Carlin Scherer, supported my research. Several Carpenter descendants have gone out of their way for me. Carpenter's great, great grandchildren, Lawrence Patrick Ives and his sisters Christine Ives Iannone and Kathleen Ives Smith sent me essential research materials, including a typed version of Carpenter's diary. Their grandfather, Emerson Ives, spent many hours deciphering the small handwriting in the tiny diaries and typing out the text. Joseph Knapp, great, great, nephew sent masses of documents and helped resolve research snags. Henry and Jack Orr answered questions on family history.

Mary Ann Kane, at the Cortland County Historical Society (CCHS), was brilliant and resourceful. Betty Bonawitz at the CCHS spent hours photocopying materials for me. Richard Beebe, the former mayor of Homer, and Bev Berry, the Deputy Clerk Treasurer in the mayor's office, assisted me. Homer's village co-historian, Charles Jermy, Jr., answered many research questions. Susannah Driver-Barstow, editor supreme gave me great editorial suggestions.

Many other historians and collection curators answered questions: Jamie Arbolino at the Senate Curator's Office; Kenton Clymer and Nicole Etcheson at the University of Texas at El Paso; Professor Emeritus at Harvard University David Herbert Donald; Farar Elliot at the House Curator's office; Eva Greguska at the Long Island Museum; Nancy Harbison at the Phillips Free Library in Homer; Harold Holzer at the Metropolitan Museum of Art; Don Huber, Supervisor of the Alton Township; Mary-Jo Kline at Brown University; Francis Lapka at the Lilly Library; Barbara McMillan at the White House Curator's Office; Alyssa Morein at the New York Historical Society Library; Libby Spaulding at the Cortland Free Library; Cindy VanHorn at the Lincoln Museum; Cecilia Wertheimer at the US Bureau of Engraving and Printing; and Christine Weideman at the Yale University Library. Finally, I am grateful to Laine Akiyama for her gorgeous illustrations, and to Seth Bongartz for seeing a book in my manuscript.

ILLUSTRATOR ACKNOWLEDGEMENTS

I must first thank Hildene for giving me the opportunity to work on this project. Everyone on staff made sacrifices in order for me to have the extra time to focus on this book and I am grateful.

To research what particular rooms in the White House looked like when Mr. Lincoln was president I looked to classic Lincoln books and collections for inspiration and reference including: *The Inner Life of Abraham Lincoln, Six Months at the White House* by F. B. Carpenter; *Lincoln, An Illustrated Biography* by Philip B. Kunhardt, Jr., Philip B. Kunhardt, III, and Peter W. Kunhardt, the Library of Congress and the New York Historical Society's collection of Matthew Brady photographs. They were invaluable resources and Marie Ferrarin's initial phone calls helped to narrow my search. Of particularly patient help to me was Melinda Smith, Associate Curator in the Office of the Senate Curator in the U.S. Capitol, who made repeated trips to the west staircase of the Senate wing to take digital photographs of Carpenter's painting hanging there. Carpenter's great, great grandchildren, Christine Iannone Ives, Kathleen Ives Smith and Lawrence Patrick Ives, were especially helpful providing scans of his preliminary sketches and photos of his diaries. So were priceless artifacts and letters gifted by great, great grandson A. George Scherer, III and his mother Carpenter's great granddaughter Clara Scherer

Whitney, thank you for the chance to work with you and for the beautiful story of a painter's passion, a friend's hope and the compassion of a great man. Lastly, I must thank Yoshi for making the greatest sacrifice, that of time not spent together and projects put on hold. You're the best.

PICTURE CREDITS

Back Cover: Hildene The Lincoln Family Home, Manchester, Vermont.

End Leaves: Unpublished letter from William Shepard Mount to his father, Shepard Alonso Mount, who transcribed this copy of the letter. Gift of Carpenter's great, great grandson, Mr. A. George Scherer, III.

Quote: By William Shepard Mount from an unpublished letter from William Shepard Mount to his father, Shepard Alonso Mount. Gift of Carpenter's great, great grandson, Mr. A. George Scherer, III.

Author's Note: Diaries of Francis Bicknell Carpenter courtesy of his great, great grandchildren, Christine Ives Iannone, Kathleen Ives Smith and Lawrence Patrick Ives.

Page 10: Emancipation Proclamation courtesy of Picture History, LLC, www.picturehistory.com.

Page 13: Engraving of Abraham Lincoln by Francis Bicknell Carpenter and Frederick W. Halpin. Courtesy of Carpenter's great, great grandson, Mr. A. George Scherer, III.

Pages 14 and 15: Study sketch for *The First Reading of the Emancipation*

Proclamation to the Cabinet by Francis Bicknell Carpenter. Courtesy of his great, great grandchildren, Christine Ives Iannone, Kathleen Ives Smith and Lawrence Patrick Ives.

Pages 14 and 15: Study sketches of Lincoln's cabinet members by Francis Bicknell Carpenter. Courtesy of The Union League Club, New York, New York.

Page 16: Study sketches for *The First Reading of the Emancipation Proclamation to the Cabinet* by Francis Bicknell Carpenter. Courtesy of his great, great grandchildren, Christine Ives Iannone, Kathleen Ives Smith and Lawrence Patrick Ives.

Page 23: Unpublished letter from Shepard Alonso Mount to Francis Bicknell Carpenter. Gift of Carpenter's great, great grandson, Mr. A. George Scherer, III.

Pages 26 and 27: Illustrations based on *The First Reading of the Emancipation Proclamation to the Cabinet* by Francis Bicknell Carpenter which hangs above the west staircase in the Senate wing of the Capitol Building.

Page 29: Self-portrait by Francis Bicknell Carpenter. Gift of Carpenter's great, great grandson, Mr. A. George Scherer, III.

BIBLIOGRAPHY

Brown, John Howard. "An American Historical Painter: Francis Bicknell Carpenter," Peterson Magazine, March 1896.

Carpenter, Francis. B. Unpublished diary, courtesy of Carpenter descendants, the Ives family members.

Carpenter, F. B. *Six Months at the White House with Abraham Lincoln: The Story of a Picture.* New York: Hurd & Houghton, 1866.

Carpenter, Frank B. "Anecdotes and Personal Reminiscences of President Lincoln," in Henry J. Raymond's The Life and Public Services of Abraham Lincoln. New York: Derby & Miller Publishers, 1865.

Carpenter, Frank B. "Abraham Lincoln: Personal Recollections and Reminiscences of a Six Months' sojourn in the White House During the Lincoln Administration," Peterson Magazine, March, 1896.

Carpenter's unpublished letters in the private collection of Carpenter descendant, Mr. A. George Scherer III.

Donald, David Herbert. *Lincoln.* New York: Simon & Schuster, 1995.

Freedman, Russell. *Lincoln. A Photobiography.* New York: Clarion Books, 1987.

Holzer, Harold. *Lincoln Seen & Heard.* Lawrence, Kansas: University Press of Kansas, 2000.

Holzer, Harold, Gabor S. Boritt and Mark E. Neely, Jr. *Changing the Lincoln Image.* Fort Wayne, Indiana: Louis A. Warren Lincoln Library and Museum, 1985.

Lorant, Stefan. *Lincoln: A Picture Story of His Life.* New York: Crown Publishers, 1975, reprint edition.

Neely, Mark E. and Harold Holzer. *The Lincoln Family Album.* New York: Doubleday, 1990.

Perkins, Fred. *The Picture and the Men.* New York: A.J. Johnson, 1867.

Turner, Justin G. and Linda Levitt Turner. *Mary Todd Lincoln: Her Life in Letters.* New York: Alfred A. Knopf, Inc.

U. S. Military Prison Alto[n]

My Dear Father;

Ill. Jany 6, 18[ ]

I have just received yours of the 2[ ]
[ ] I also received a letter from you dated Dec. 25
[I] should have been answered long ago, but a severe
storm has so blockaded the rail road that no mai[l]
been sent from here for nearly a week; but to da[y]
[bel]ieve the mails are running regularly. I have n[ot]
[ ] heard any thing from my release. I have no dou[bt]
[t]hat it will be forwarded to me shortly. You expr[ess]
surprise in your last letter at my not having be[en release]
[ ]ed by the commander of the Prison. I would say th[at accor]
[di]ing to present orders from Washington he would no[t be]
[per]mitted to release a prisoner of war upon takin[g the oa]
[o]th, without a special order from head quarters;
[thi]s the reason I have not been released before this-
[w]eather has been extremely cold here for the past
[ ] so cold that I have been obliged to stay in the hou[se]
[ ] all the time. I have lived in the sunny South, s[o long]
that I cannot stand the cold as I used to. A larg[e]
[crow]d of Rebels arrived at this prison a few days ago.
[the] cry is still they come. I pray to God that the da[y may]
soon come when this d—d Rebellion will be [stamp]
[ ]d out, and the last Rebel camp fire crushed ben[eath the fe]
[e]t of the Union Soldiers. Then, when the Stars & Strip[es]